ONE SANE ONE

China's Newest Colony: America

JASON ONEIL

authorHOUSE

AuthorHouse™
1663 Liberty Drive
Bloomington, IN 47403
www.authorhouse.com
Phone: 833-262-8899

© 2023 Jason ONeil. All rights reserved.

No part of this book may be reproduced, stored in a retrieval system, or transmitted by any means without the written permission of the author.

Published by AuthorHouse 02/14/2023

ISBN: 979-8-8230-0113-7 (sc)
ISBN: 979-8-8230-0114-4 (e)

Library of Congress Control Number: 2023903020

Print information available on the last page.

Any people depicted in stock imagery provided by Getty Images are models, and such images are being used for illustrative purposes only. Certain stock imagery © Getty Images.

This book is printed on acid-free paper.

Because of the dynamic nature of the Internet, any web addresses or links contained in this book may have changed since publication and may no longer be valid. The views expressed in this work are solely those of the author and do not necessarily reflect the views of the publisher, and the publisher hereby disclaims any responsibility for them.

CONTENTS

Introduction vii
Books by the Author xi

Think Note 1   Executive Orders 1
Think Note 2   China's Plan 5
Think Note 3   Energy Policy 12
Think Note 4   Climate Change 16
Think Note 5   Big Tech 21
Think Note 6   Christianity 26
Think Note 7   Work Ethic 29
Think Note 8   Employee Unions 34
Think Note 9   School Boards 38
Think Note 10 Racism 43
Think Note 11 Urban Decay 48
Think Note 12 Farmland 52
Think Note 13 Infrastructure 56
Think Note 14 Vietnam War 59
Think Note 15 Modern Warfare 63
Think Note 16 Foreign Affairs 68
Think Note 17 Tipping Point 73

INTRODUCTION

At the Constitutional Convention in Philadelphia in 1787, delegate Benjamin Franklin is reputed to have said when he left the Hall: "You've got your republic…if you can keep it!"

Franklin, a student of history and very wise man, knew that a republic dies due to incompetent leaders, unfulfilled promises to the citizens or both. In essence, the key to survival is an informed electorate which applies common sense based upon confirmed facts to make good decisions. This is probably why Franklin was a newspaper man. He believed in reporting the facts in order for the citizens to make informed decisions.

In the mid-1900's in America, a young Norwegian man was drawn to journalism. His name was Eric Sevareid. He was an avid student of American history. He was keen to understand the rationale behind the Constitution and the genius of the men who conceived it and made it a living document capable of sustaining a free-enterprise Republic. Franklin and Thomas Jefferson were two of Sevareid's heroes. He modelled many aspects of his own thinking after their written words.

Initially a cub reporter in Minneapolis, the young man was "conscripted" as a reporter for CBS in Europe covering World War II. Later he covered the war in Vietnam where on one occasion he had to be rescued from the jungles of Cambodia. His CBS colleagues saw the potential for this "truth-seeker" at the same time that the television evening news hour needed a dose of sanity to interpret the world's events.

The Dane, essentially a shy, introspective person, was thrust into the limelight as a commentator on Walter Cronkite's daily News Hour. It was during the turbulent decade of the 1960's and early 1970's when tens of millions of new viewers tuned into the broadcast to learn the news but also the sane truth of Sevareid's twice-weekly, 400-word, two and one-half minutes of much appreciated truth serum about the meaning of global events. Eric Sevareid's guiding principals were simple: 1) trust in a knowledgeable citizen 2) guided by the lucid sanity of the Constitution, the greatest document on Earth since the Bible.

As a Marine Officer in Vietnam, I would lead resupply convoys to the fire bases in the norther sector of the country. After a mission, I would return to a compound and watch the war unfold on television. Sometimes our units were the subject of the broadcast about the "progress" in Vietnam. I knew that the generals and politicians were lying. There was no way we could win against a guerilla revolutionary force. It reminded me of America's struggle to be free from England. There was no way America would contain the Chinese-backed forces in Vietnam.

Commentator Sevareid had experienced it first-hand. He knew the truth and reported it, much to the dismay, indeed anger, of the Johnson Administration. Like several of my fellow officers, I went into combat as a brandishing Eagle but returned home as a singed Pigeon! Five long years later, Saigon would fall. Over two million Vietnamese and 50,000 Americans died because of the lies.

Today, a half-century later, Washington is again spuing lies, huge ones, about all aspects of our society. History has shown that democratic societies routinely die after 250 years, most before that. The root cause is that the central government can not meet a society's demands. Today, Washington has almost finished its creation of a Socialist State over the silent protests of a hapless Republican minority.

This book attempts to apply Sevareid's sane techniques to describe the sad tragedy unfolding before our eyes in a manner which the reader can apply real-world experience to form an opinion about the impact of current events. Perhaps, a ground swell will lead to a revolutionary zeal capable of regaining our republic from the Marxists and their millions of recruits who are blind to the role that China is playing in the internal destruction of our democracy prior to their planned peaceful takeover of America, a goal which must be achieved to gain world domination.

BOOKS BY THE AUTHOR

Bald Eagle Vision
The Red Box
Turbopod
Turbospace
Sinecure
Cyberclipper
When Baldie Cries
New Age Ark
A Necessary Coup
Micronations
Hypersonica
Mission Embryo
DroneViper
Bald Eagle Vision 2
DragonChip
Cellphonica
Solarmania
Escape from La-La Land

Mirachip
Tough Sale
Padlockers
Flipphonia

Think Note 1
EXECUTIVE ORDERS

The American Constitution does not address in detail nor prohibit a President from issuing Executive Orders (EO's). They exist to fundamentally address a need to modify an existing law which is exercised elsewhere in the Federal Government. It can be used by the President to justify emergency action without Congressional debate and/or funding. This was the case in the 1930's and 1940's when President Roosevelt issued over 300 EO's to end the Depression and wage World War II.

Recently, a president has used dozens of EO's to nullify a previous administration's actions while creating political support for the Democratic Party.

Clearly, the EO is both a strategic and tactical tool. However, as we'll learn, the jury is out about its legitimacy in a democratic republic. Our Constitution creates three separate but equal branches of the Federal Government as a check and balance system on behalf of the citizenry.

It's worked well for 250 years. Congress represents the public and manages the purse. The judiciary implements the Rule of Law and affirms the meaning and intent of the Constitution. The Executive Branch administers the bureaucratic tasks essential for effective governance of a free society. And this branch has cabinet positions for department leadership. In the last half-century, presidents have created key cabinet positions for Health, Environment, Energy, Homeland Security, Transportation and Veterans Affairs. These departments must be effective in meeting the demands of the citizens. If they are not, the void is traditionally filled by Socialist promises.

Advocates of the liberal use of the EO point to the transparency-meaning publication of the EO by print or digital media. This assertion is blatantly false because the public never reads an EO. Newspapers almost never publish them. The result is the avoidance of any public debate, much less compromise, about the substance and requirement for an EO. The legislature never participates in the process. As a result, EO's which profess to be temporary to deal with a crisis, such as take control of an industry, usually end up as "pseudo laws" implemented by the bureaucracy. Almost a century ago, President Roosevelt routinely issued EO's. Major topics covered the depth and breadth of the nation such as:

- Seizing control of the manufacturing of war material such as petroleum, food and the railroads
- Social Security Act
- Conservation: Dams, Parks, Beaches and Public Lands
- Veteran's Issues (Over two dozen EO's)
- Bureaucracy: Creation of Agencies, Boards, Committees, and Councils
- Foreign Affairs: Proclaimed the neutrality of the USA from Europe's war. Also included the freezing of Japanese and Chinese assets
- Finance: Took control of silver and gold; created and opened new banks

By the end of World War II, dozens of permanent organizations had been created which still exist today and perpetuate a dependence upon the Federal Government by tens of millions of citizens.

Most recently, on the first day in office, the president issued 17 EO's. All but two terminated programs initiated by the previous president. Several related to climate and global warming issues. Sixteen of the seventeen were purely political to harvest votes for the Democratic Party to insure long-term incumbency. Huge sums of money had to be printed to fund the initiatives during a period when the nation couldn't even pay the interest on the National Debt.

Recently, White House spokespersons have floated the idea of an EO to create Central Bank Digital Currency (CBDC). Informed financial analysts point out this is an attempt by the government to exert total control over people's money. In other words, the Federal Reserve and National Bank would be authorized to take money out of people's accounts to implement monetary and fiscal policies.

This act, along with a new Digital Identification for tracking citizens, would doom the democracy. In essence, the current government is saying: "your actions, money and whereabouts aren't really your business." The state owns you as a commodity to further its goals, all of which constrain human freedom. Such an EO could be signed, and Joe Citizen would not know the full impact of Government by Edict, often labelled: "Marxist-Socialism."

So, fellow countrymen and women, be very mindful of the impact of the EO's upon you and your loved ones. They may not be unconstitutional. But they have a permanence capable of altering the republic forever. One only needs to visit Beijing China to see this process in action today. Such a controlling action by a political party could very well require another Revolution to avoid the deliberate assault on our freedom.

Think Note 2
CHINA'S PLAN

On September 29, 1959, the Premier of Russia, Nikita Khrushchev, had a sober warning for America. In a well-publicized speech, he warned that small doses of Socialism over time would ultimately result in the Republic becoming a Communist state. He said this in perhaps the most perfect period in the nation's history, July 1953 and October 1963, just before President Kennedy's assignation. Cuba became a Communist outpost in this hemisphere, but missile exchanges were averted. Since then, Russia has focused its expansion on neighboring countries.

But, today, seventy years later, the premier's forecast is coming true, indeed, almost complete. And the irony is that the very country America tried to "contain" in Asia has been responsible for the unabetted march toward Communism in the land of the Bald Eagle. America must soon (somehow) overcome the following actions highlighted by Khrushchev:

- Healthcare cost
- Poverty
- National Debt
- Gun Control
- Welfare programs
- Education
- Religion
- Class Warfare
- Media Control

The Chinese know that a nuclear exchange would end life on Earth. Consequently, since the Civil Rights Act of 1964, the Asian dragon has spent trillions of dollars to assure the death of America's free-enterprise democracy. And, as mentioned in Think Note 1, Digital ID and cryptocurrency are on the near horizon if the Democrats are successful in their implementation. In essence, this is the Social Credit System (SCS) already implemented in China to completely control the 1.4 billion souls.

So, let's review the actions, which together, will end our Democracy unless another American Revolution takes place, this time between opposing political parties and philosophies.

First, the health of the average American has seriously declined since that perfect 1950-1960 period. Cancer, diabetes and obesity are rampant. Fentanyl made in China coming through Mexico is ruining urban America. And, with the Chinese-made Covid-19 virus, Washington conditions the public to national lockdowns. Suspect vaccines are no match for the viral mutations. In large measure, China will inherit a very sick, aging population.

Bad health contributes to and is an outcome of the next takeover action: Poverty. Poverty is rampant when millions of jobs disappear to China, and the work ethic disappears leaving legions of homeless and pitifully poor on the streets. As a result, the government pours trillions of dollars into the economy which helps few and worsens the national debt. One-fifth of the debt is owed to China. Uncle Sam can't pay the interest, much less the principal. Prolonged default on payments would lead to Depression in which China would assume ownership of whole industries for pennies on the dollar.

Premier Khrushchev's fourth predicted event was Gun Control. Today, virtually all the headlines are about the use of guns. The administration calls for gun control legislation. They say they want to stop the slaughter. But the real reason for gun control via confiscation is to avoid an assault on the Democrats in power.

In America today there are over 80 welfare programs from assisted housing to school lunches and dozens for "free" programs for the masses. Forty-eight million souls exist on food stamps. These programs are not going away.

They are a major contributor to the debt and personal dependence upon the government for survival.

The Chinese respect scholars. Education is a key element of a person's youth. Consequently, China invests heavily in all levels of the American education system. It funds teachers unions to teach anti-American curricula. It denigrates our history to fuel racism in order to tear the country apart. The Constitution is ignored. And while this is happening, a quarter-million Chinese students at our universities often take our technologies back to the mainland on thumb drives.

Another of Khrushchev's warnings was Religion. In America today, polls show that about 90% of the citizens proclaim an affiliation with a religion. Yet only 12% attend services regularly. There are too many convenient excuses not to go to a service, regardless of the denomination. This is precisely what Communist regimes require: the state fills the void in the absence of God.

When was the last time you were branded a "racist." The label is a key component for a central government to start and maintain class warfare, the 8th item in Khrushchev's speech. Racists can't complain about high taxes to pay for the welfare programs. They must remain silent and accept Washington's "leadership."

All of the above characteristics of a Socialist society are amplified by a complicit media. China has bought the movie studios, movie chains, social media companies and graphics software companies to ensure that no negative report about China in broadcast by any means. The daily newspapers ignore this political corruption while fanning class warfare. They are megaphones for the Socialist agenda at the expense of the very people pay for the newspapers, the middle class.

In addition to the above tools, China has another important tool to further its plan. It's the very heart of a democracy, the election. Chinese operatives at the state capitals have been very successful to help legislatures enact laws which:

— Push the mail-in ballots
— Eliminate proof of a person's identity
— Increase non-citizen voting
— Minimize audit systems and ballot counting

And, finally, they pay runners to harvest ballots at low income housing projects and health facilities of all kinds. Of course, the ultra-liberal social media in print and on-line has supported these actions. Indeed, criticism of the processes is "modified" (meaning "eliminated") from chatrooms. In essence, the election is over by the time the televised debates take place.

The Democrats are also well funded by "outside sources" to push the Green New Deal agenda requiring trillions of dollars. This initiative is an overt attempt to squash America's petroleum industry with solar and clean alternative systems, all of which are made in China. Even electric vehicles further China's takeover ambitions by relying on items made in China and the Supply Chain to get them here. And, while legions of scientists debunk global warming, the Chinese use it as a weapon supported by the social medias.

The modern tragedy is that the Republicans have not successfully opposed this growth of Socialism. The silent majority has been silent due to incompetent leadership and the racist rhetoric. And these Socialists are quickly morphing into Diehard Communists. And history will show how the Democrats lose control of the situation and are forced to vacate the District of Columbia by Totalitarianism.

So, what's the solution? It's not complicated. Indeed, it's quite simple. A conservative champion must lead America's Second Revolution with a battle cry that Americans are hostage in their own nation. Socialist politicians must be "ushered" out of the Washington swamp. An interim government lead by seasoned, non-tech, businessmen and women must create work projects which do not benefit China while abiding by the Constitution and Bill of Rights. Few revolutions are successful. The odds are horrible. But the Great Experiment called America, required nothing less than a new constructive, compassionate social order based upon individual freedom and the Rule of Law. Even a one-legged Bald Eagle is still atop the food chain. Will that person(s) please come forward.

Think Note 3
ENERGY POLICY

Energy is necessary for life, even if it's just to stay warm or cool. Whether from the atom, oil, gas, sun or wind, the control of energy is the control of society. The country's future is directly dependent upon its energy supplies and policies for their use.

Today, countries are using a Green New Deal (GND) policy to justify measures to replace petroleum as the primary energy source. All energy sources must be "clean" in the future. As a result, a government funds solar and wind initiatives regardless of the cost and utility for an economy. And all of the components of the system-solar panels, wind turbines, batteries, charging stations and requisite cables are made in China.

The U.S. Department of the Interior estimates the volume of undiscovered, recoverable oil in the lower 48-states to exceed 150 billion barrels. In addition, there's Alaska, dozens of off-shore rigs, tar sands in Utah and shale deposits in Pennsylvania. The total number of gallons is incalculable. And this is before natural gas and coal enter into the equation.

Energy enables every industrial activity. It is required to plow, plant and harvest food, run transportation systems, build structures and wage war. Petroleum is the basis for chemicals, drugs, metals and almost everything a human can touch. So, why is the current American president so set on replacing it with new "clean" sources? Why must everyone drive an electric vehicle? The answer is simple and quite tragic. The Democrats want to wean the public off of fossil fuel in order to create a lower standard of living which levels society and makes the citizens more dependent upon Washington for existence. It's methodically implementing, perhaps unknowingly, a totalitarian state.

In addition to stopping the Keystone Pipeline from Canada refusing drilling applications and land-use leases, Washington is draining the Strategic Petroleum Reserve. This rush-to-green agenda is making life unaffordable for millions of citizens. The Big Drain temporarily lowers gas prices at the expense of potential drastic consequences in the future.

The Green New Dealers are fanatics who dictate major Democratic policies. They blame the petrochemical industry for every atmospheric ill including global warming. This is contrary to the fact, as supported by thousands of scientists, that the planet is not warming due to man-made causes. Indeed, it is in a cooling period lasting hundreds of years. And, most recently, the Democrats want to ban gas stoves due to a report in part funded by the Chinese. Corrupt data distorts the impact of residential gas stoves on childhood asthma. It also bans gas stoves in restaurants because of the possibility of a miniscule release of nitrous oxide. Given the total lack of irrefutable evidence, the multi-trillion dollar infrastructure would be abandoned even though natural gas is cleaner and cheaper than alternatives.

It is an inconvenient truth that Climate is an anti-Capitalist tool which began to be applied in the West in the 1960's. The pursuit of net-zero emissions will destroy Western economies. China gives unwarranted legitimacy to the GND. The country has never been concerned about Mother Earth. It's all about a slow death for America's energy independence while China's 5-year plan calls for the construction of 250 new coal-fired electric generation plants!

The Chinese are doing this because it will make America a third-world country. And why do the Chinese do this? It's simple: without petroleum, America can't wage war. So, what's the solution. It's painfully clear that a new administration will have to implement new policies which include but aren't limited to:

- Repeal ALL of the Democratic Executive Orders
- Restart the Keystone Pipeline
- Issue Oil and Gas exploration permits, even in Wildlife areas
- Stop the buildout of Wind Farms
- Bring solar panel production back to this country
- Provide tax credits for energy research and development, including cleaner gas and quick-start electric ranges
- Defund the GND initiatives which do not bring jobs back to America
- Eliminate the Department of Energy. (Other Think Notes discuss in detail about this incompetent bureaucracy filled legions of disguised unemployed who obstruct, not support sane energy policies.)

All of the above policies are aimed at accomplishing two goals: 1) Reduce, delay and, if possible, eliminate the potential of a Chinese takeover and 2) Create a prosperous, sustainable, compassionate and affordable life style while creating an undefeatable adversary for China.

Think Note 4
CLIMATE CHANGE

In December, 1997, in Kyoto, Japan, an international agreement was signed by dozens of nations. Over the following decades, climate scientists warned about the Inconvenient Truth that the Earth is warming, and human behavior is a significant factor. At the same time, 31,000 scientists signed a digital proclamation that there is "no convincing evidence that humans can or will cause catastrophic heating of the atmosphere." Indeed, they point of many long-term studies which prove that the Earth is actually cooling.

A few observers said that "the climate hoax is a tragic way to continue research grants and even tenured university appointments." However, over the last four (4) years, it has become alarmingly clear that the Green New Deal is a smoke screen hiding $10 Trillion worth of carbon avoidance overreaction, and worse yet, a vehicle for social engineering in large measure funded by China. China is using climate as a weapon against America, It's another way the Communist Party redistributes wealth in order to control a society.

Conservatives sarcastically label the flurry of Congressional bills as the New Raw Deal. They point to the goal of 100% energy from clean, renewables as unattainable while devastating the petroleum industries to kill the republic's free-enterprise economy. They welcome repairing the infrastructure, providing smart power grids, reducing air pollution from public transportation and the pollution of water from farming. But the legislation is a Trojan Horse of Socialist promises which guarantee employment at a fair wage, free medical care, paid vacations, housing, food, energy and education for a lifetime.

One of the key technologies promoted by the Greenies is solar energy. It's a clean way for a homeowner to show his or her support for environmental issues and enjoy a four-year payback period. The fundamental problem is that it takes more energy to produce them than they ever deliver to the customer. The impact is still a sales job because the overall carbon release is not reduced. And many critics call the technology a massive scam because of dozens of related problems like leaking roofs and future inability to sell a property. Solar panels aren't allowed in landfills. So, the long-term impact remains unclear.

However, as questionable as solar energy may be, wind mills are a proven environmental and economic disaster. What started as a novel industry in northern Europe, has become a nightmare in America for both the owners and the investors for the following reasons:

— Offshore lease rights are sold at exorbitant prices guaranteeing an unprofitable venture
— Tax credits are being phased out

Transmission lines to the shore are extremely expensive to build, lay, maintain and replace

— The electricity is sold at uncompetitive prices
— Salt water environment requires costly maintenance every six months (A fact which is left out of every investment prospectus.)
— Decommissioning costs are never told to potential investors
— Third generation wind mill is 853 feet high (that's an 80-story building!) and an offshore eyesore
— The current technology has reached its limit with no increase in power generation
— A wind farm can never generate more than 5% of a region's total electricity needs
— Windmills require massive battery facilities for electricity storage

And if that isn't enough for a no-go decision by a government entity, the massive pieces can not be transported on the highway and are not accepted in landfills. All of this and the fact that the total component manufacturing processes produce many times more greenhouse gases than conventional coal burning electricity generation plants with advance chimney scrubbers.

Perhaps the shining light for the proponents of clean energy is the electric vehicle or EV. While expensive to purchase, even with federal subsidies, they are fun to drive and offer advance safety features. What is conveniently overlooked, however, is the massive electrical infrastructure necessary to support thousands of charging stations required across the country. To put this in perspective, it takes a railcar full of coal to create enough electricity to keep the EV on the road. Replacement batteries cost more than a comparable new car! And, like the windmills, the old batteries are not accepted at landfills.

So, who is the big winner in this Green Movement? It's not the American consumer. It's China. Virtually ALL of the parts of ALL of these systems are manufactured in China using electricity from coal-burning plants. The rare Earth elements required by the batteries are dug up and refined in China. In addition, the Chinese have a large lobby of American firms in Washington seeking subsidies in the name of job creation---job creation which primarily occurs in China.

So, who's the biggest loser in this struggle to use climate change as a vehicle for social change? The answer is tragically simple: America. The nation is being transformed into a totalitarian state one battery at a time. Conservative objections are not loud enough for this Inconvenient Truth to be discovered and the folly stopped before another Bald Eagle is slain in flight.

Think Note 5
BIG TECH

Look around and you'll see that 85% of Americans own a smart phone. Sixty per cent say its "my most valuable asset." Americans are addicted to, indeed trapped by, the release or a newer, more capable device with cheaper storage and creative applications such as video streaming and wagering. Today, 7 million American men are on the Internet all day. They are not working. They are in digital La-La Land spending time in non-productive tasks. "I hide in my video game while someone else takes care of my needs."

That "someone else" is the Socialist central government whose every action is aimed at keeping the citizen, and now 50 million people not born in this country, dependent upon Washington. This is precisely the situation for which the Chinese CCP has worked so diligently. So, how pervasive is this addiction? Here are some revealing statistics:

- Over one-half would save the cell phone first in a house fire, before the family pet!
- Two-thirds have texted someone in the same room or car
- One-half spend more time on the phone than with their significant other
- One-half feel stressed if the smart phone is lost for more than 30-minutes
- Almost 100% feel compelled to answer a "ping."
- On average, Americans check their phone once every four minutes. And that includes the youth doing their homework.

So, it's time to reflect on who's behind this social revolution and the long-term impact on our country. The microchip has made this American invention possible. It empowers a handheld device capable of telephone calls, emergency alerts, television and a countless number of Internet-based applications. It's the primary news media rather than the printed newspaper. It an entire techie culture centered in Cupertino, California at the Apple Headquarters. This Silicon Valley has seen the growth of corporate giants or "Big Tech" create and manage digital platforms with hundreds of millions users. The Chinese-owned Tik Tok is one of these giants.

ONE SANE ONE

What began as a mobile device for convenience has morphed into an entertainment necessity and political bullhorn with anti-Constitutional censorship never before seen in history. In essence, with direction from the Democrats in Washington, Big Tech-the bastion of ultra-liberal political philosophies-takes orders as to who can chat or post an opinion. Just like conservative politicians are banned from college campuses, their views are banned from the digial space. It's a win-win scenario for Washington, Big Tech and, you guessed it, China. Why? Conservative ideas and policies are never broadcast via the various media. As a result, the public is not educated about:

— The Constitution
— Free enterprise economy
— Rule of Law
— Federalism
— Balanced Budget
— Bill of Rights and 2nd Amendment freedoms
— Impact of Welfare, Racism and the loss of the Family Unit

The conservative minority will always remain a minority as long as their views are 'moderated' by Big Tech.

And it gets worse, much morse, when the platforms use Artificial Intelligence to create "Deep Fake" videos to sway public opinion. A citizen forms an instant opinion which is reinforced by Government legislation, Executive Orders, civil suits and press conferences, all reinforced by the big city media companies and even Alexa at home. So, in essence, Big Tech erodes democracy precisely at a time in history when its subscribers need to hear the truth about China's intentions and millions of American-designed social media weapons made in that country.

So, what can we do?

We could do nothing and hope that a severe national crisis forces Congress to act against this censorship. But since this censorship benefits the party in power, nothing will get done. Any Bill would die in committee. Perhaps a group of conservative governors could petition the Supreme Court to render a decision which prevents Big Tech from this moderation practice because it is unconstitutional. A constitutional Convention could be called where three-fourths of the states would be required to amend the Constitution. This would take years while Big Tech develops more sophisticated means of moderation via AI which more effectively limits conservative discourse.

So, the only avenue left for the Conservatives may be to play by the Democrat's rules and "get out the vote" to unseat the democrats and change the laws and neutralize certain Executive Orders. Given the damage inflicted by Big Tech's growing social media influence in national and state politics, (Big Tech executives pour hundreds of millions of dollars in local races!) the conservative control of Congress can't come soon enough. Without a change in leadership, the Socialist lies will be propagated by Big Tech which ultimately will lead to unfunded welfare programs and social disasters which even the Big Tech billions of dollars will not be able to prevent.

Think Note 6
CHRISTIANITY

The decline of Christianity is best put by the American millennial proclaiming: "Oh, yeah. I'm a Catholic." What he or she really mean is that they were raised a Catholic but haven't been to church in years. And, all too often, this means they are too afraid to renounce the faith experienced during youth. The following statistics highlight the decline:

— Two-thirds (64%) of Americans, ages 18-35, doubt the existence of God. This statistic doubled in the last generation.
— Six difference research polls confirmed the retention rate at 67%. This means one out three raised to be faithful have left Christianity and now assert no religious affiliation.
— The decline is in all three essential areas: membership, growth and attendance

— This is a global phenomenon: In Germany, 500 churches have closed since 2006. Canada has lost 22% of its churches over the last decade. Most of the buildings have been converted into restaurants and breweries. In Ireland, 85% identify as Christian. However, the youth want abortion and same sex marriage legalized. New priests are not being ordained.

— In America, Christianity is the largest religion with a 20th Century high of 91% of the total population in 1976. This has declined to 64% in 2020. Weekly attendance in Catholic churches is now 20%. The number of priests has dropped 50%. Only 1% of the nuns is under the age of 40. The other denominations are also experiencing similar declines. Less than one new religious structure is being built for every four that close.

So, what's the reason some churches remain vibrant and are able to welcome members? The short answer is leadership and social issues. They have community outreach activities, special programs for millennials and social events for seniors. They remain silent on same sex and abortion issues. And, finally, the clergy issue a positive message as opposed to: "You're going to burn in Hell!"

Why is it important that congregations grow one family at a time? It is because China's Communist leadership has its own religion: "Obey me, or I'll send you and your family to the Lithium mines." Afterall, they are the new God who needs the mineral to make batteries for the clean energy movement.

So, the loss of religion is filled by the tragic lie of Climate/Global Warming. Hundreds of millions of new believers use this anti-Constitutional alliance of church and state to justify wholesale social change in the name of equity. Imagine Al Gore in sainthood.

Think Note 7
WORK ETHIC

"Nobody wants to work anymore!" This is the lament of employers across America. The country has had the strongest work ethic in the world for over a century. On average an American would work 230 more hours per year than a European. Vacation periods were one-half as long. Then came the Chinese pandemic, and everything changed. Combined with millennials growing up in the digital age, an at-home social media mentality swept the nation. It was largely enabled by the American Rescue Plan which issued $749B in weekly payments. These payments combined with over 80 welfare programs-everything from childcare to college tuition-enabled the millions of Generation X and Baby Boomers to remain at home in the digital La-La Land of nonproductive isolation.

Today there are over 13 million jobs available, but applicants aren't showing up for the interviews, even via Zoom! Millennials age 18-33 do not feel the need to have a Work Ethic. Increased wages, the highest in American history, aren't enough to move over seven million out of their parent's house for a 9 to 5 job.

Europe demonstrates the dismal impact of a declining work ethic. Government's ever-expanding entitlements create a huge tax burden needed to support the "caring" Socialist governments. It's become an invitation to laziness and fraud. The reality has not been faced: Entitlements don't reduce poverty or improve the mobility and job prospects of potential workers of all ages---a working parent does. That person creates a product or service which multiples the creation of more jobs. It's Economics 101.

Part of the tragedy is that a government's unemployment statistics cover real stagflation, inflation and recession. There is no job creation. The statistics are misleading. An unemployment rate of 5% is actually 3% because of who dropped out of the workforce. And why not? A family of four in America today gets on average $72,000 per year in federal entitlements. In this scenario, a videogame is much more important than a job. As a result, the vaulted American work ethic declines at an accelerating rate forcing more and more shop owners out of business.

So, when we talk about this personal quality called "Work Ethic," what do we really mean? Work ethic is a belief that work and diligence have a psychological, moral and socio-economic value both to the individual and society. Believers feel it is essential to meet goals. It's a set of principals which helps achieve a consistent, high-quality product and/or service. It's a source of self-respect and fulfillment. Characteristics include:

— Personal positivism
— Rewarding routine
— Conscientiousness
— Availability & Reliability
— Goal-oriented performance

In general, work itself reinforces self-reliance, the time-value of time, delay of gratification and a higher valuation of leisure.

In the business world, a frequent maxim is: "How hard you work determines how far you'll go up the scale of recognition and the accumulation of wealth." Ben Franklin claimed that the Bible revealed to him the virtue of hard work. On the other hand, anti-capitalists believe: "hard work deceives the working class into becoming loyal servants of the elite."

In America today, economic decline fosters a negative work ethic, accelerated by government handouts, which focuses on self-centered perks and distance from the workplace. As a result, remaining in La-La Land is more important than learning a trade which will enable self-sufficiency in the future when the government runs out of our money.

To regain a positive work ethic in America will not be easy. It's a lot more than changing corporate structures and culture to please the millennials. Some required steps include:

— Phase out many of the gargantuan welfare programs
— Alter the liberal arts college curriculum to focus on high-grade trades (There is plenty of money for training programs.)
— Create massive national infrastructure projects so sorely needed around the country. Today, for instance, there are over 300,000 highway and railroad bridges in need of repairs. These programs require team work and goal completion leading to work ethic reinforcement. The individual accomplishes tasks which generate energy to do more. In essence, the American laborer applies the vaulted work ethic for both personal and national benefit. This process enables each person to reject a dependence upon a Socialist state which promises an idyllic nirvana of a non-work culture. This violates Economics 101 instruction and can't be sustained. China has over a million people in concentration camps extracting rare-Earth

minerals for the battery production process to pay for the "care" of the masses. A healthy work ethic helps a person avoid such a plight and ultimately rejoice with: "I did that!"

Think Note 8
EMPLOYEE UNIONS

In America in 1983, 20% of the workforce was unionized. The brotherhoods were established to ensure workers had the right to "a living wage earned in a safe environment."

Now, four decades later, the number has dropped to 10%. Of the 14-million members, one-half are in the private sector and one-half in the public sector. And on average, non-union median weekly income is 80% of union take home wages or $48,000 versus $60,000. Current union demographics tell quite a story:

— Union membership is primarily sought for health insurance and retirement packages
— Union membership is high in local and state jurisdictions at 41% primarily for firemen, police and teachers
— The industries with the lowest union membership are finance, computer science, farming and sales.

Farmers have fought unionism for centuries. And salespeople so frequently change jobs that paying dues to multiple unions becomes a non-starter.
— Blacks are union members more often than whites. For many reasons, black organizers have a much easier job of convincing a person to join. "We're on your side against White Management."
— The age group 16-24 has the lowest union membership. They are new to the workforce and have not started families where saving money is a foremost consideration, much less retirement funds.

Ninety-six per cent of all employers in America have less than 50 employees. In small business, unions have a hard sell because the owners know that unions make it more difficult to fire someone. Consequently, today's union leaders focus on large businesses like Starbucks and Amazon because of their published profitability. The leaders focus in negotiations: "That's our final offer. Take it or leave it!"

Seventy-seven per cent of Americans back the concept of unionism as a legitimate workforce requirement. Routine surveys reveal the public attitude that "unions have a positive effect on the economy." And it's not a surprise that 74% of Democrats and 34% of Republicans support unionism. Every four years, the Republicans argue that union demands drive jobs to China.

Over the last decade, unions have come under attack in two important economic environments: teaching and government employees. In both cases, the unions are criticized as being arms of the Democratic Party. Teachers unions across the nation bully school boards to take action contrary to the will of a large number of parents in a district. Anti-American courses laced with CRT, EQUITY and WOKE are being forced upon school districts, and any objection is branded as "racist."

Around the Washington, D.C. beltway, there is a quiet but growing anger amongst non-government employees that the union members are the best compensated workers in the world. They don't need a union to extract more very costly benefits from the taxpayers outside the beltway.

For better or for worse, private and public unions are here to stay. According to the rules of the national Labor Relations Board (NLRB), the decertification of a union takes a majority vote of the membership. Even publicized corrupt union leadership is insufficient to close a local union. The loss of one's benefits far outweighs any decertification initiative.

In the debate of the value of unions in today's economy, there is one thing where scholars agree that union leaders are ignoring: Work Ethic. This is particularly the case for government unions. Unless the union member is working on a political campaign, there is no urgency to work more efficiently or effectively.

Since conservative unions don't exist, Republican leaders at all levels of society need to advance more constructive affordable solutions to current national problems in order to neutralize the inherent advantages the Democrats enjoy. And unions are a powerful voice for Socialistic programs. China can use the union bosses as generals in the totalitarian army. The primary weapon against such a future is to bring jobs back from China which give workers hope for sustained, future benefits based upon a company's imbedded work ethic which leads to profitability in our free-enterprise economy.

Think Note 9
SCHOOL BOARDS

In America today 91% of college students graduate with ultra-liberal, "Semi-Socialist" political philosophies. They are brainwashed by professors and teachers who have never had to make a payroll. They can spew venom about the American way-of-life and never be held accountable. The students are infected with half-truths about our country's founding and the leaders who made this experiment happen.

Today, these graduates are teaching in primary and secondary schools around the country. Polls reveal that even after decades of teaching, the liberal philosophies are still part of the instruction. Consequently, they are influenced by the social views dictated by the Teachers Union. These unions are largely beholden to the Democratic Party for funding to perpetuate these liberal views. An "inclusive curricula" is required by the 13,500 school district boards in the country. The teachers present the material as the truth. They can't question the assertions or historical interpretations for fear of being fired and losing their pensions. Some worry if their homes will be firebombed.

It's in this environment, where the money trail demands compliance, that the Chinese can accomplish what the CCP proudly calls: "Dominance, Diversity, Duncing and Distance." A review of these "4-D's" is useful to understand the full impact of the School Boards on America's youth.

— Dominance. Democratic candidates for the school board endorsed by the Teachers Union win three-quarters of all political races. So, the Democratic socialist agenda dominates the lesson plans. There is no rebuttal; it must be taught.
— Diversity. "Diversity" is typically a synonym for "racism." Diversity means that youth of color are more equal than white students. Key components of this direction is Critical Race Theory (CRT) and EQUITY (not equality) where blacks deserve more today because of slavery by our forefathers 275 years ago. In addition, "WOKE" or "wake up to demonstrate against whiteness" and the New York Times' 1619 Project which demands reparations be paid to the black for the slavery. Any negative comments about this direction are labelled "racist" which bullies any conservative objection into stone-cold silence.

- Duncing. This is "Dumbdowning" fostered by the school boards. A student of color is routinely behind the standard learning curves. Consequently, in Baltimore for instance, only 12% of high school seniors can pass the standard mathematics examination for graduation. It's so bad the teachers must resort to "EthnoMath" where 2 and 2 can be 5 or anything the student wants it to be. Duncing ignores cursive writing—another strike against the youth. Gifted students are prohibited in many urban school districts. Exposure to genuine intellect is not tolerated by the dominating school boards.

It's tragically clear that because of this non-learning and/or wrong-learning environment, millions of urban youth are dependent upon Socialist handouts the rest of their lives. The Chinese leadership smiles at the prospect.

- Distance. It refers to a lack of adult leadership for the urban students of color. Typically, the student is from a one-parent home where the parent is earning subsistence wage and is distanced from the student so homework goes undone. Even if the student is given a laptop for distance learning, there is no discipline to log onto a Zoom session. The laptop becomes a Gameboy console. So, in reality Duncing begins at home.

The above tragedy is perpetuated by a federal Department of Education. For the last half-century, thousands of these educators rise to key positions in the department. Hundreds of billions of dollars are spent only to witness the tests scores plummet.

The above Report Card clearly shows a failing grade. But it gets worse; much worse. New subjects replace the "Three-R's" of "reading, righting and rithmatic." Starting in second grade, the students are immersed in anti-white instruction along with gender fluidity where little girls can be boys, and boys can have their penis removed without any social stigma.

School boards, all 13,000 of them, have the elected authority to change the above ugly reality. The problem is there is NO will to do so because of the teacher's liberal, slanted education and bullying by both the Teachers Unions and the Department of Education. Therefore, the school board pays "lip service" to:

— Focus on student achievement
— Strategic use of resources
— Monitor progress with real data to take corrective action

— Employing new, non-prejudice, learning technologies
— Ensure smaller class size

The most critical school board responsibility—connecting with the community to ensure a quality education—is absent. Indeed, Parent Teachers Association (PTA) meetings are a waste of time. And school board meetings are strictly structured to preclude parent objections.

Democracy is sustained in large part by a discipline at home to provide an education to better one's lot in life. The education system reinforces the Work Ethic necessary to succeed in the workplace. Each worker contributes to the free-enterprise system, which along with the basic freedoms guaranteed by the Constitution, perpetuates the Republic. The elimination of this basic education is a key tenant of Communism. And given what's happening in our urban school districts, the future grown ups will be ripe for indoctrination by Beijing. Who will tell today's parents that THEIR Marxist future will not be a happy one because the school boards control our youth?

Think Note 10
RACISM

America is the least racist country on Earth. Black slaves were imported from Africa to plant and harvest rice and cotton during the 1700's. The American Constitution gave each citizen rights in a system of justice. But it wasn't until the 1860's that the slaves were emancipated. Then, in the first half of the 1900's, whites and blacks had to share foxholes in World Wars, Korea and Vietnam. Although not fast enough for some people, America's diversity movement helped blacks move up to the highest levels of society, even to the Presidency.

Our founding fathers though our diversity would be a strength. Some thought it would doom the new Republic. Diversity itself is not the problem. But diversity without commonality leads to social division. Once this happens, the fight over "who gets what" inevitably begins.

The first black President, Obama, unfortunately created and/or endorsed a steady stream of false claims that America was an inherently racist society with a biased judiciary and law enforcement system. Obama rekindled racial factions which had been steadily disappearing in America. Several polls confirmed that over 60 per cent of Americans felt that "race relations had gotten worse under his administration."

Today, Obama's vice president, Biden, became president in some measure because of his black, female running mate. So, today, tragically more than ever before, the nation's leaders incite this division for political gain to keep the social-democrats in power in order to freely implement their Socialist agenda. It appears unknown to the administration, the Chinese Communists have hundreds of initiatives in process in America to peacefully absorb the new Socialist state into their global empire.

The Biden/Obama Regime has methodically employed the following social weapons to ensure racism is a smokescreen to obscure their new Socialism:

— WOKE: Afro-American slang to "wake up to the prejudice." It is used by corporate America, Big Tech, educational institutions and government agencies to ensure that everyone understands that black lives matter, more than the white majority.
— EQUITY: This WOKE ideology that there is inequality between the races. It means that racial

groups are not standing on an equal footing. Equity is not equality of opportunity but equality of the result. In other words, whites and blacks must be leveled in every statistical measure, a key tenant of Marxism. An example of this is the banning of single-family homes in the suburbs in favor of high-rise housing blocks where everyone is equal.

— CRITICAL RACE THEORY (CRT): This "theory" is really an ideology which rejects the U.S. Constitution by casting aside the Bill of Rights and prevents free speech and religious freedom. It is an ideology which must be taught in America's schools where students are taught that they are different because of race. It is actually a form of racism such that discrimination and racism become the solution to discrimination and racism! Anyone who does not embrace the ideology is branded a racist. There is no middle ground in this deliberate levelling of society.

Recently, CRT is a prerequisite in the leftist-controlled Federal government. Workshops are held at the FBI and DHS. In the Treasury Department staff members are taught: "all white people contribute to racism." It's how urban riots are justified. So, in city squares around the nation, statues are pulled down because they represent the inherent evil of whiteness.

How is this possible on the least racist country on Earth? First, a recent Gallop Poll showed that 77% of conservatives are afraid of speaking for getting blasted by social media, or worse, firebombed. Second, the CRT argument is a mousetrap where disagreement is evidence of a racist. And, third, the fact of slavery in America is undeniable, and, therefore, white atonement is long overdue. Period.

So, how does America fulfill Martin Luther King's proclamation "judge people by their character, not their skin color." The answer is simple but increasingly more difficult to implement. The process must include:

— Stop identifying people by color and ethnicity
— Ban the Box; Government will not ask for this data on forms
— No government policy will be based on race
— No diversity training in the Government, including the military
— No federal funding to colleges and universities which use race as an admissions criteria
— No recruitments will be based upon racial quotas

And the bottom line is that our country must strive to promote equal opportunity for everyone but will not guarantee equal outcome, a critical tenant of Communism. Indeed, soon, perhaps sooner than we want to believe, the rioters demanding payments for past actions, will welcome the Chinese, only to be jailed. How's your Chinese language skills?

Think Note 11
URBAN DECAY

In America over 45,000 people are killed by guns annually. Study after study report that the reduction of handguns does not reduce this crime. Eight million new small arms and 15 billion bullets are made every year around the globe. They are very portable between countries. Today, 30 states allow citizens to carry weapons in public. Twelve states allow concealed guns to be carried after rigorous background checks. And legislation which bans guns runs amuck of the Constitution.

In Baltimore, 94% of high schoolers have heard gunshots. Forty-two per cent have witnessed a shooting. Shootings close businesses and/or deter new ones in the neighborhood. Jobs are lost. And the availability of handguns increases the suicide rate in all demographics. The root causes for gun violence are many and complex. It's more than just availability. And it's more than adding policemen on the corner.

ONE SANE ONE

The rapid decay of America's great cities is a systemic problem in large measure funded by the very politicians who pay lip service to the reduction of violence. It's a series of many vicious cycles which must be broken before urban youth have some prospect for a happier future.

The first cycle which must be broken is the lack of competent, effective assistance from Washington. It's a tragic truth that minority representatives in Congress do very little, if anything, for the citizens of their urban district. They get into the Swamp in D.C. and do everything to remain in office, often at the expense of their own districts. Funding for programs and facilities does very little to increase the chances of minority children realizing the American dream. Wholesale change in Congress is required to break the dependence upon welfare, improve the education, bolster the work ethic and prove that "racism" is only a tactic to bully the opposition.

In major cities like New York, Los Angeles and Chicago, incompetent Democratic mayors devote one-quarter of the annual budget to fighting crime with dismal results. No major city is safe at night. Baltimore, known as "Charm City," is a classic example of a medium-size city loosing population to a lethal shooting or "failed murder" every day. Whole empty row houses become "crack" houses. The city hall is dysfunctional. Symbolic of this is the District Attorney who perceives her role as releasing felons from captivity so they rob, rape and kill again. The city officials are a laughing stock just sitting in place waiting for that unearned retirement check.

In this urban nightmare is another cycle which must be broken: incompetent school systems led by Democratic school boards and Teachers Unions promoting racist divisions. Far too few resources are devoted to technical education sufficient to give students the possibility of a good paying job.

Roadside billboards with the message: "Use a gun; go to Jail" have little impact upon the crime rate when the tragic cycle of fatherless homes can't be broken. More babies are born out of wedlock to garner more welfare. There is no effective role model to instill a positive work ethic so homework assignments go undone. Without a future, the youth turn to drugs and guns for a lifestyle, however short.

The situation grows dire when the police departments don't have the resources and WILL to fight crime comprising the bulk of the evening news on television. More highly-trained officers are required in the worst districts. And the quick response to an unlawful act is required.

One novel solution is to equip an Emergency Response Command Vehicle with a cannister of "Nanowasps." These miniature, multi-function drones can be package by the dozen in a roof-mounted cannister. Each Nanowasp can have a different function to include but not be limited to:

- Excellent photo resolution from 500 feet
- Direct SWAT and K-9 team deployments
- Direct Firemen and First Responders
- Support disasters with medicines, ropes, lifejackets
- Pursue felons indoors; warehouses
- View hostage situations
- Deploy oil slicks and tetrahedrons to pop car tires
- Release tear gas and smoke grenades
- identify and shut down illegal drones

One novel application is the use of Sound Grenades which emit a 130+ decibel sound to temporarily debilitate a fugitive or mob with vision blurred and balance lost such that the person(s) crumples to the pavement. Selected individuals are then easily apprehended for the appropriate legal prosecution. The cannister can also be mounted on a helicopter or speedboat.

The Chinese involvement to hasten the urban decay is quite obvious and the subject of other Think Notes. What has to happen soon, however, is the creation of well-funded and competently-led programs to break the above cycles. It will take many years to repair the damage to the city and the people caused by a callous neglect of duty by bureaucrats, often from one political party. Without such goal-oriented programs, the "Charm" of Baltimore will be lost forever.

Think Note 12
FARMLAND

America is blessed with the richest farmland in the world in the central valley of California. Iowa and surrounding states have over six feet of topsoil. These regions are at the same latitude as the farmland in central China. The difference is that only about 50% of their land is arable due to deserts, pollution, pest infestations and sprawling urban areas. As a result, the CCP has initiated a trillion dollar global campaign to buy the land, technologies and foodstuffs necessary to feed 1.4 billion people a day.

Today, American farmers are asleep on the combine as the Asian dragon breaches the wall of the U.S. Department of Agriculture to pull off the largest heist in farming history. China has entered every facet of America's farming industry to own land, machines, software and the labor necessary to ship products back to the mainland.

Over the past decade, China has appropriated (a kind word for "stolen") trillions of dollars of sophisticated U.S.

technology with a particular focus on agriculture. It's so flagrant and urgent that U.S. customs authorities have nabbed "mainlanders" attempting to transport pilfered corn, wheat, soybean and rice seeds to China. The arrests have been ignored while Beijing loots American farms and agricultural laboratories. The United States Intelligence Community, all 19 agencies, have focused on Russia while China is a threat to national security many times greater.

China is desperate for more farmland. And the country is intent on cataloguing seed and DNA on a vast scale. The country's number two import is soybeans and committed to providing food security for its people. Recent, ChemChina, paid $46B for Syngenta gaining access to transgenic seeds and crop protection products. It's part of an all-costs movement to acquire agricultural technologies. If the seeds wont grow in China, they are planted in vast parcels acquired around the world. To put it in perspective, economic espionage cases with leads to China at the FBI have jumped 1,300% in the last decade.

Further proof of China's desperation is the 350,000 acres of rich farmland recently purchased by the CCP and its front companies. And one agricultural purchase which has made the headlines is Smithfield, the largest pork processor in the world. Over 33,000 hogs are slaughtered in the Tar Heel Plant in North Carolina every day! In addition, thousand of live hogs are shipped to the mainland as part of their food security program.

The magnitude of the efforts has finally forced Congress to act. A recent Bill, Promoting Agricultural Safeguards and Security Act of 2022 (PASS) prohibits the following countries from major land and corporate acquisitions: China, Russia, Iran and North Korea. Backroom discussions revolve around the fact that America has its own problems feeding urban children.

There are 360,000 Chinese students enrolled in U.S. universities, many of which are land-grant institutions with extensive agricultural research programs. If only 1% are spies, that's 3,600 data-gathering informants on U.S. soil. As part of the CCP's permission to study here, the students are obligated to bring home thumb drives and seeds, if possible.

At these schools are Confucius Institutes and Chinese Students and Scholars Associations (CSSA's). These organizations exist to educate Americans about the Chinese history and society. In reality, they can be fronts for spies, all paid for by the American taxpayer with grants to the educational institutions. In essence, we are paying to deteriorate our own food security while strengthening our primary adversary.

To make matters worse, the CCP has a global recruitment program called "Thousand Talents Plan." It exists to steal data, technology and researchers and agricultural experts. Thousands of researchers have grants and research projects to aid Chinese agriculture, again paid for by the U.S. taxpayer. The talent recruitment program funnels the research into the fields of China and provides food for its military.

So, given the severity of this hidden problem, what must be done? Here is a partial list:

— Close the Confucius Institutes
— Forbid the sale of land and agricultural companies to China
— Severely limit Chinese student enrollments in agriculture schools
— Stop CSSA funding
— Conduct "at school" seminars to educate the staff on the nature and methods of this "Grand Theft."
— Increase the U.S. Customs enforcement powers and personnel to deport suspects immediately, complete with confiscation of all digital devices

The above actions can be formalized in a Presidential Order which alerts the nation to this security problem and authorizes observers in the Fields of America. Imagine. We're helping to grow food to feed their military and aid China's security program. This nonsense must stop.

Think Note 13
INFRASTRUCTURE

What if you turn the water spigot, and no water comes out? You may not be in a third-world country. You could be in one of three-dozen urban areas in America where the century-old pipes no longer can flow water. And today the American Society of Contract Engineers (ASCE) estimates that one-half of the 300,000 bridges in America are over 50-years old and need repair. Even the newest roads are useless if a bridge doesn't overcome an obstacle.

When one looks around at our aging infrastructure, there is no shortage of projects which are already overdue:

— Power stations: coal, oil, gas and nuclear
— Roads, railroads and runways
— Dams and waterways
— Public buildings; Railroad stations
— Hospitals
— Power transmission towers and related infrastructure

- Ports and supply chain depots
- Military bases

And thousands of crumbling factories which saw their production move to the Orient.

So, while so much attention is given to "smart, green" infrastructure like windmills and smart highways, the infrastructure necessary to go "Green" deteriorates beyond commercial profitability and utility. The Green Revolution will NEVER produce more than 9% of the nation's energy requirement, yet huge budgets are earmarked for the technologies. This must stop.

So, what's the solution to the problem which gets more urgent every day? It's a three-point program which will cost trillions and take a couple of decades to complete:

1. Create a Project Selection Committee which must prioritize:
    - Public Security: Power, roads and bridges
    - Food Security: Farming and distribution systems
    - Medical Security: Facilities and Drugs
    - Cyber Security: Automated systems of all kinds
    - Job Security: training and new industries to create over 20 million, non-union, well-paying jobs with family-sustaining benefits.

2. Create an Infrastructure Development Corporation (IDC). This is a Federal organization staffed by riffed Department of Homeland Security (DHS), Department of Energy (DoE) and Department of Education (DoED), Commerce, EPA and unneeded bureaucracies which are simply disguised unemployment. Focus on downsizing the military and train the personnel for long-term infrastructure employment. Why do this? America is not the world's policeman. Communism does not need to be contained; ultimately it will die on its own. And aircraft carriers can be used for the steel to build bridges.
3. Focus on the Energy Industry. Restore pipeline projects, new shale extraction, and modernize gas-powered plants with coolers to provide more efficiency. The energy will be a major component of the factory modernization projects which build the infrastructure components. New facilities will be used to bring jobs back from China. Closed military bases will be the personnel and logistics centers for the nearby projects.

A national focus will be required to employ tens of millions of Americans with a zeal similar to the World War efforts. The country will need the new transportation and production facilities to remain competitive in world markets, a key factor in getting the nation's debt under control.

Think Note 14
VIETNAM WAR

Over the last century a form of government has taken over a major portion of humanity. It's called Communism where all souls share a "common" future. It's a militant Socialism where the central government owns all the means of production, indeed, all of the citizens as well. Today, almost two billion people live under a Communist regime, primarily in Russia and China. Here, in the West, Communism is compared to a malignant tumor which continues to spread. It is the complete opposite of America's free-enterprise democracy.

After World War II, Russia tried to spread Communism into Europe. During the 1950's, China attacked Korea. While safe in this hemisphere, American politicians developed a policy called "Containment." The goal was to prevent Communism from infecting other nations in what was called "the domino effect." Leaders in democratic countries were appalled at the living conditions and lack of individual freedoms in Communist countries. It developed into a Cold War of containment.

The region of Vietnam, Cambodia and Laos, called Indochina, was a colony of France for a century. The French coveted the teas, spices, rice and rubber. In 1954, a North Vietnamese army under General Ho Chi Minh and supported by China defeated the French forcing their withdrawal from the region. America's containment policy "forced" the country to send advisors to ascertain the ability of the South Vietnamese to repel invaders from the north. This began a fateful 20-year period of warfare against the North Vietnamese (Vietcong) by the United States and a handful of allies.

For a decade the poorly trained and low morale troops of South Vietnam defended their territory as the Vietcong grew in size, built defenses, dug tunnels and received new weapons and training from Russia and China.

In 1965, U.S. Marines landed at the Da Nang airbase to defend it from assaults from the north. This was just the beginning, and the human cost of the war was tragic:

— 1-3 million North Vietnamese dead
— 250,000 Cambodians and 60,000 Laotians dead
— 58,000 Americans dead (Over 225,000 wounded)

And even today, 50-years later, thousands of Americans suffer from injuries and mental trauma from the losing effort.

So, how did this happen, and what are the lessons for future generations? The fundamental truth was that America had never fought a true guerilla war where the enemy is all around but invisible. America's generals thought that an overwhelming firepower could bring the Vietcong to the peace table. They were wrong. Indeed, during the decade of the heaviest fighting, America's generals lied about the win probabilities.

This was the first war to be televised in prime time. Walter Cronkite's Evening News had expert commentary by Eric Sevareid, who openly but very tactfully, questioned the progress and, more fundamentally, why America was there at all because our homeland was never at risk.

As the war wore on and the U.S. exhausted so many strategies with 63 million tons of bombs, daily aircraft sorties and battleship broadsides, it was clear that the Vietcong were not going to be defeated. As the generals kept requesting more men and bombs, protests at home grew on over 1,300 college campuses. Late in the war, U.S. soldiers massacred over 500 villagers in My Lai. The leader, Lt. William Calley, was court-marshalled in prime time on television. It brought out the worst of war.

In late 1974, the South Vietnamese government crumbled and by early 1975, the Vietcong were on the outskirts of the capital city of Saigon. In April, the last 900 Americans and Vietnamese sympathizers were evacuated from the roof of the embassy by helicopter. Within five months, Vietnam, Cambodia and Laos were Communist countries.

So, what did America learn from the only war it ever lost?

War is Hell, and Guerrilla War is Really Hell. Defense of the homeland wins every time. Wars fought on television activate public opinion, for or against a government's policy. Congress needs to review every General's request for more troops. There is a direct correlation between increased casualties and decreased support at home. Because of chemicals and emotional trauma, the impact is felt in hospitals decades later.

Finally, if Russia or China wage military campaigns today on allies or neighboring countries, what will Uncle Sam do? Given the huge backlog of domestic problems, the odds are bullets and band aids will be provided but the Marines will remain aboard ship. The American Bald Eagle will only fly over this hemisphere.

Think Note 15
MODERN WARFARE

Today in America one question is never answered by the Congress or the White House: Why do we spend three-quarters of a trillion dollars annually on Defense when new technologies make conventional warfare obsolete? The combination of hypersonic, stealth and Artificial Intelligence can make a single strike so debilitating that the mere threat of a repeat can dissuade an aggressor.

The question must be answered so the American taxpayer can refute the folly of archaic General Officers and Admirals, the number which must be drastically cut by at least 75%.

Today's world demands homeland attention and action, not a global police force. The world's policeman needs to retire because of what's happening here:

— Deep recession caused by unjustified trillions of dollars expenditures

- Inability to pay down the National Debt
- Outmoded Monroe Doctrine; America does not need to protect this whole hemisphere
- No credible threat from a foreign military
- Open border which must be closed and a structured path to citizenship enforced
- Idiotic Green New Deal expenditures which have no basis in science and directs funds to welfare programs
- Youth which loves war only in video games

So, what's the answer to this deep crisis which could easily topple our Republic? It's a simple answer which will take years to implement: Focus on homeland defense. Period. Here are some actions which will assure our national safety, the Federal Government's primary reason for existence.

First, in this cyber era, America must develop an advanced cyber virus/worm capable of debilitating a country's automated systems. The worm would be broadcast over a target by an autonomous, stealth, hypersonic missile. The virus spreads automagically when workstations are opened. A Trojan Horse deletes the machine's hard drive while simultaneously filling the remaining space rendering a military or civilian control system powerless. Everything from aircraft carriers to power stations are rendered useless.

Fortunately, this virus can only be neutralized by U.S. commands. Only one small demonstration is probably required because the following threats are very real:

- Close an electrical grid(s)
- Open dams
- Release prisoners
- Steal government documents
- All of the above and hundreds more

So, after only one small demonstration, a counter attack, is considered by an adversary to be futile. Local supercomputers would never be able to find a defense against our worm. A demand for total disarmament of offensive weapons by our country would be met in short order given the prospects of another worm which could be catastrophic.

Such a weapon would allow America to focus on our homeland with a long list of priority projects starting with the drastic reduction of one-million government employees. The Department of Homeland Security (DHS) will be the first to be padlocked. It was a knee-jerk reaction to 9-11 with phony missions staffed by legions of incompetent bureaucrats. And a new Defense Department will be focused on our soil, not foreign lands with one-fifth the current budget. The bureaucrats and soldiers will be trained for roles on the multi-trillion dollar infrastructure modernization projects.

The Space Force can't be justified and will be eliminated. The need for 4,000 helicopters goes away, and the aircraft inventory will be dramatically reduced and mothballed. Other new era actions will include:

- Military academy attendance will be cut by 60 per cent
- Aircraft under construction will be halted, and no new platforms will be authorized pending security reviews
- 95% of the Recruiting Offices will be closed
- The Intelligence Community will be consolidated from 19 agencies down to 6, and they will have 50% staff reductions
- 50% of the Embassies will be closed with tasks moved to Regional Consulates
- 60% of the Navy vessels gets drydocked with many cannibalized for steel for the infrastructure projects
- The nuclear stockpile is dramatically reduced as verified by international watchdog entities

The above actions are considered essential in order to avoid financial default and social anarchy as the nation tetters on the tipping point toward Communism. Our

Constitution creates many safeguards for our property. War destroys property. Now, with a limited demonstration of a cyber weapon, conventional and nuclear warfare should cease to be relevant. Given the eliminated Federal government largess, the next generation will have the resources, and hopefully the Work Ethic, to construct the vibrant, compassionate republic envisioned by our founders.

Think Note 16
FOREIGN AFFAIRS

Ever since the Spanish-American War in 1898, America has served as the world's policeman. The goal was to stop conflicts from spreading to our shores. The nation's foreign policy was based upon the Monroe Doctrine which told the rest of the world: "hand's off this hemisphere." During World Wars and regional conflicts, America drew its sword to contain Communism while spreading Democracy.

Recently, over the last quarter century, American foreign intrusions have been costly with horrible results. Uncle Sam invaded Iraq under the pretense that Hussain was developing nuclear weapons. None were found, but troops were stationed to protect the oil supplies.

Based upon the worst intelligence in the nation's history, America abandoned Afghanistan after ferreting out terrorists for two decades. Intelligence agencies reported that the country's military could last 2-3 years after a withdrawal. It lasted just THREE DAYS before an extremely well-provisioned Taliban-ISIS terrorist state was created.

On the home front, the Democratic Socialists rapidly assumed total control of the citizens through Covid-19 lockdowns and Global Warming initiatives. The petroleum industry was being gutted. The predicted outcome came true: the worst American economy in 90 years with one-third of the population dependent upon handouts from Washington. Indeed, famous historian, Victor Davis Hanson, recently didn't recognize America for over a dozen reasons including election laws, civil riots, military incompetence, transgenderism, rampant inflation, weaponization of the FBI and blacks demanding retribution for slavery. Any counter arguments, however sane, are branded "racist." The unstated goal was to cancel the Constitution. Today, the nightmare continues. So, imagine how bad things must be in other countries for millions of people to risk life and limb to come here.

So, hopefully it's not too late to initiate an INTERNAL Containment policy closing bloated, ineffective Federal Government departments. In this regard, several books have been written about padlocking or dramatically downsizing-several Federal departments. One such candidate is the Department of State (DoS). It has been largely hidden from public view like the Intelligence Community while creating an incompetent, bloated bureaucracy. How did this happen? Some of the primary reasons include:

— Distance. DoS sites are a long way from the cub reporters of American newspapers. Local papers relegate foreign affairs to the back section.
— Nepotism. Once a family member enjoys the huge salary, free residence and global travel benefits, the whole family wants a career there.
— Bureaucracy. DoS grew to cover most of the 190 countries on Earth. As a result, the annual budget has grown four-fold to $66B in just two decades.
— Management. Every department manager has had to increase staff annually by bureaucratic maxim.
— Construction. In the name of security, new multi-billion-dollar embassies have been constructed around the globe. Whole campuses in Europe and Japan have stood empty for years while the taxpayer pays the rent.
— Employee Unions. They exist to extract more benefits for one of the most pampered workforces on Earth. The unions still remain a potent force against automation to reduce headcount.
— Rewards. Ambassadorships are coveted by thousands of senior government officials in Washington. The overseas posts must exist to

fill this political need. Imbedded in the DoS is a special project office for retired officials to check on telecommunications systems at embassies and consulates. These systems are fully automated and monitored from America. There is no need to travel to the site. But legions go, often performing top secret missions.

All of the above money pits would make a nationally-televised expose. The good farmers of Iowa would be rightfully mad!

So, what's the solution to this mess? Several steps taken by a new president might include:

— Recognition that the policeman role is no longer viable, much less worth huge sums of money
— Drastic reduction in DoS mission areas such as Climate, Health, Alliances, Equity, Counter-terrorism, trade policy and human trafficking.
— Reduction in annual payments to International Organizations by at least 50%. After a century, it's time for other countries to step up to their financial obligations.
— Reduction of classified, clandestine missions and services

— Reduction in the headquarters by 25% over 4-years while new, proven automated systems provide secure on-line services
— Prohibition of offloading of DoS services to federal contractors in order to keep oversight organizations intact
— Hiring practices are greatly enhanced with proven, relative experience and language skills for viable candidates

Finally, it is obvious that a new Cost-Basis management cadre is required in this department. The padlocking must be a successful component of a Balanced Budget Amendment to the Constitution. This doesn't mean that America totally withdraws from regional programs and/or problems. But the foreign policy and military disasters like Vietnam, Iraq, Iran and Afghanistan must not be repeated.

An efficient, focused DoS could serve as a leader in a new national effort to thwart China's takeover of the Republic. Indeed, without such leadership, the new Communist state would tragically be unrecognizable by Professor Hanson and a couple hundred million free-loving souls.

Think Note 17
TIPPING POINT

"Dad, that was really cool. I'm glad we came. Thanks," said Evan as the 16-year-old and his father crossed the esplanade on the east side of the U.S. Capitol building.

"Son, let's sit down on that park bench and take a moment to reflect on what we just experienced in the Visitor's Center," said the seasoned journalist with four decades of experience reporting events in Washington, D.C.

They sat down and took a couple sips of a sport drink when the Reporter Sevareid pointed and said, "Evan, look! There's a Bald Eagle perched on top of the Statue of Freedom on top of the Capitol dome!"

"Dad, you're right. I can even see his white head with my binoculars. How symbolic!"

"You're right, my son. And I bet he's pretty disgusted with what he sees!"

"Huh. What do you mean?"

"Well, remember in the movie when Ben Franklin emerged from the Continental Congress and said something?"

"Yes, something about the Republic."

"That's right. "You've got your republic, if you can keep it."

The father then looked up at the bird, paused and said, "Well, Evan, it's a real tragedy when America, the Great Experiment in Democracy, is on the verge of dying. And I believe that Baldie up there on the dome senses it."

"OK, Dad, what's this all about?"

"Well, the Bald Eagle, the supreme winged raptor on top of the food chain, senses that our democracy is at the tipping point toward extinction. My professional experience tells me the same. Unless the nation's politics and society change soon, real soon, nothing can continue our proud 250-year experiment."

"Dad, what do you see that I don't?"

"Son, your future may be very ugly, not like the wonderful life style your mother and I have enjoyed. It will be really horrible. Daily life will be a real challenge with no hope for the future."

"Dad, I'm all ears!"

"Well, it doesn't take a genius to see what's happening and the forces behind it. I'll give you a snapshot so you can ponder it, even do some research on your own."

"You know, I learned how to research questions and problems from you. I'm pretty good."

"Yes, I know. See if you remember this. In 1964, the Civil Rights Act was passed. It was the Democrat's unofficial start of the welfare state to garner low-income voters for their party. It began the downward spiral to a Socialist State. And now, as we've talked in the past, the Chinese are slowly, but effectively, turning this socialism into their brand of Communism."

"Dad, wait a minute. Do you mean that both you and Baldie see the death of the Republic on the horizon?"

"Exactly. Think about it. America is about the freedom to carve your own destiny. Millions come here for a chance. I'm living proof of the opportunity and very, very thankful. My profession has allowed me to see the truth that the "Great Society" isn't great after all. And like every Socialist regime in history, it's bound to fail because it can't keep false promises. In the meantime, the citizens (or should I say "slaves') have a miserable existence. The leaders only want followers to keep them in office, not to flourish and have a stake in the success of the country."

The father paused again to look at the eagle through the binoculars.

"The entitlement state bankrupts the treasury and the person. Small communities die in favor of urban ghettos. The "Race Card" always shuts down the opposition so the not-so-loyal minority is silenced. Senior bureaucrats have more power than the representatives in Congress. Dark money comes from Big Tech and media companies to preserve the status quo. A credible, competent opposition candidate can't win an election under these circumstances."

"OK, Dad, the situation is ugly. So, who's behind it, and what can be done?" asked Evan as he again looked at the regal raptor.

"Well, son, as you know, I've written a lot of Think Notes about our society which has changed so dramatically in my lifetime. Over the last half-century, China has been implementing its global control strategic plan. It can't be done without conquering America. They know that a military attack will not work. So, the Communist Party has been molding our society in their likeness from within. Unknown to most Democrats, the CCP has been using their Party as a principal mechanism to have our republic ultimately come under their control. Nothing is by accident. And new technologies which are invented here, like the cell phone and the Internet, become weapons against us."

"Dad, no wonder Baldie is so concerned."

"Precisely, But let me be more specific and list some social weapons which have the nation at the tipping point. Some of these weapons include:

ONE SANE ONE

— Debt Trap: America owes China trillions of dollars which can't be repaid. Our country is the collateral.
— Green New Deal: China's attempt to end our petroleum-based economy and global independence. All of the equipment for solar, wind and batteries is made in China. Our jobs are gone, and if they ruin our petroleum industry, we can't wage war.
— Fund and support the move toward a National ID and Cyrptocurrency to ensure full control of all of the citizens and their money.
— Devalue the Yuan in order to weaken the dollar in international markets
— Create viruses which kill millions of Americans, flood the country with masks and related equipment and support Washington's call for lockdowns to control the citizens
— Support corrupt School Boards and Teachers Unions which infect the youth…like you…with racist lies.
— Buy movie studios and media companies to censor any negative press about China
— Support initiatives to reduce a belief in God to be replaced by the state
— Buy key farmland and agricultural companies
— Support the destruction of urban America

I could go one, Evan. But you see how serious this is, and why our society is being "levelled" by a poor economy in order to force the public to exist on entitlements controlled by Washington.

And let me be absolutely clear about a critical point. The Chinese-American community is exemplary in its intellect, initiatives, work ethic and regard for the laws. They are the brightest students in school and the leading software engineers. It's the Communists who also threaten their lifestyle!"

"So, Dad, what's the solution? What steps must be taken now so Baldie once again proudly soars over a free and prosperous republic?"

"Evan, in my opinion it will take a revolutionary Administration which proclaims: "There is no free lunch in a Democracy!" Therefore, entitlement programs and Federal Government departments will be severely limited and/or eliminated. The focus must be on China, and we'll thwart the takeover by:

— Strong, dollar-based, reduced debt economy
— Bring Asian jobs home with next-generation products made in modern factories
— Revamp the school curricula toward democratic principals

— Modernize the infrastructure with materials made here
— Regain energy independence; bury the Green New Deal

And we'll protect our country with cyber science which creates products which debilitate foreign economies to preclude warfare. Nuclear weapons are too dangerous to use in the new cyber world."

"Dad, that's very creative. Will it work?"

"Son, it has to work! Sanity must prevail! After all, we need a safe, free and prosperous country for you and your family (and all those millions knocking at the door) in order for you and yours to fulfill their full potential."

Baldie left his perch and flew right over the two tourists who looked at each other and nodded their understanding that the tipping point might just be avoided.

www.ingramcontent.com/pod-product-compliance
Lightning Source LLC
Chambersburg PA
CBHW020453220526
45464CB00002B/970